ISBN 978-0-332-74311-0
PIBN 11236902

Abstract

(118) NO. 64-129 M (61 Ill. App. 2d 118)

IN THE

APPELLATE COURT OF ILLINOIS

SECOND DISTRICT

A. W. TAYLOR, Plaintiff - Counter defendant, vs. EDWARD MONROE, Defendant - Counter plaintiff.	)	Appeal from the Magistrate Division of the Circuit Court of Winnebago County.

MR. JUSTICE MORAN delivered the opinion of the court.

This is an appeal from the Circuit Court of Winnebago County, Magistrate Division, under Supreme Court Rule 36-1. The appellee neither filed briefs nor appeared for oral argument.

The plaintiff, A. W. Taylor, had an oral agreement with the defendant, Edward Monroe, to paint two bedrooms, an office and hallway belonging to the defendant. In addition to painting, the plaintiff was to furnish the materials and agreed to do the complete work for the sum of $262.00. The plaintiff's testimony reveals that he, with the assistance of an employee, spent seven days in accomplishing this endeavor; however,

A. W. TAYLOR, Plaintiff - Counter defendant, vs. EDWARD MONROE, Defendant - Counter plaintiff.	)	Appeal from the Magistrate Division of the Circuit Court of Winnebago County.

MR. JUSTICE MORAN delivered the opinion of the court.

This is an appeal from the Circuit Court of Winnebago County, Magistrate Division, under Supreme Court Rule 36-1. appellee neither filed briefs nor appeared for oral argument.

The plaintiff, A. W. Taylor, had an oral agreement with the defendant, Edward Monroe, to paint two bedrooms, an office and belonging to the defendant. In addition to painting, the plaintiff furnish the materials and agreed to do the complete work for the sum of $262.00. The plaintiff's testimony reveals that he, with the assistance of an employee, spent seven days in accomplishing this endeavor; however, there was a conflict in the evidence as to the actual number of days spent by the plaintiff and his helper. During this time the defendant and his family resided in the home. After completion of the work, the plaintiff's employee called upon the defendant one evening and requested payment under the contract. Begrudgedly, the defendant paid him $75.00, but refused to pay the balance of $187.00. A small claim was filed for the balance due and on the day of hearing the defendant appeared and orally filed a counterclaim in the sum of $200.00 for damages. The defendant testified that the walls were improperly painted, the carpeting was covered with paint, as well as the woodwork and the furniture. In addition to the testimony of the defendant upon his counterclaim, the president of the local painter's association testified that the job was done in an unworkmanlike manner and it would be necessary to spend between $400.00 to $450.00 in rectifying the damage caused by the plaintiff.

The magistrate at the conclusion of the evidence and arguments of counsel held for the plaintiff on his claim and against the defendant on his counterclaim. It is from these judgments that the defendant appeals.

The first contention for reversal is that since the plaintiff did not do his job in a good workmanlike manner, he has not fully performed his contract, and, therefore, cannot recover because of a breach of contract. While this is a good rule of law, still it was the magistrate's duty after hearing all of the evidence to determine, since the evidence on this point was conflicting, which side to believe. The magistrate decided in favor of the plaintiff. For this Court to hold to the contrary, or to hold that his decision was against the manifest weight of the evidence would there was a conflict in the evidence as to the actual number of spent by the plaintiff and his helper. During this time the defendant and his family resided in the home. After completion of the work, the plaintiff's employee called upon the defendant one evening and requested payment under the contract. Begrudgedly, the defendant paid him $75.00, but refused to pay the balance of $107.00. A small claim was filed for the balance due and on the day of hearing the defendant appeared and orally filed a counterclaim in the sum of $200.00 for damages. The defendant testified that the walls were improperly painted, the carpeting was covered with paint, as wel as the woodwor and the furniture. In addition to the testimony of the defendant upon s counterclaim, the president of the local painter's association testified that the job was done in an unworkmanl ke manner and it would necessary to spend between $4 0.00 to $450.00 in rectify ng the damage caused by the plaintiff.

The magistrate at the conclusion of the evidence and arguments of counsel held for the plaintiff his claim d against the defendant on his counterclaim. It is from se judgments that the defendant appea s.

The first contention for reversa is that since the plaintiff did not do his job in a good workmanlike manner, he has fully performed his require an opposite conclusion to be clearly evident. Hulke v International Mfg. Co., 14 Ill. App. 2d 5. The record in this case does not so warrant.

The defendant next argues that where the value of services received exceeds the contract price, and no fraud is involved, it does not relieve a party from performance of his contract. This is true. However, the defendant bases this argument upon the written combination of a memorandum of decision and order of the magistrate dated December 1, 1964, which was appended to his brief as "Annex A." The notice of appeal herein was filed on September 14, 1964; the praecipe for record was filed September 24, 1964; the approval of the report of proceedings was dated November 3, 1964. Nowhere in the record or abstract does this order appear. What does appear in the notice of appeal is that the defendant is appealing from an order of July 17, 1964. Consequently, this argument is not properly before this Court and cannot be considered by us. People ex rel. Drury v Redd, 243 Ill. App. 521.

The judgment of the Circuit Court of Winnebago County is affirmed.

JUDGMENT AFFIRMED

Abrahamson, P. J. and Davis, J., concur

49889

MITCHELL J. ALSTER,	)	(6 I.A. 163)
Plaintiff-Appellant,	)	APPEAL FROM
vs.	)	CIRCUIT COURT,
CHICAGO TASTEE-FREEZ CORPORATION and ALVIN D. ROSE,	)	COOK COUNTY.
Defendants-Appellees.	)	

MR. JUSTICE MURPHY DELIVERED THE OPINION OF THE COURT.

Plaintiff appeals from an order which struck Counts II and III of his third amended complaint and dismissed Chicago Tastee-Freez Corporation and Alvin D. Rose "as parties defendant herein, with prejudice." The determinative issue is whether the absence of an express finding by the trial court "that there is no just reason for delaying enforcement or appeal" renders this order not appealable under section 50(2) of the Illinois Civil Practice Act.

The record indicates that Chicago Tastee-Freez Corporation, of which Alvin D. Rose is president, entered into an agreement with plaintiff on March 20, 1962, whereby plaintiff was to operate a store at 1058 West 87th Street, Chicago, for a period of ten years, for the purpose of engaging "in the sale of Tastee-Freez products" from said premises. Three documents were executed: (1) a "Tastee-Freez Operator's Agreement," for a period of ten years; (2) a "Sub-lease" for 1058 West 87th Street for the term "commencing on the 15th day of March, 1962, and expiring on the 30th day of April, 1964, inclusive"; and (3) a "Conditional Sale Contract" for equipment to be used in dispensing the "Tastee-Freez" products.

Plaintiff commenced operations on March 23, 1962. Under date of August 29, 1962, plaintiff received a letter from "Chicago Tastee-Freez Corporation," advising plaintiff that "unless you live up to this agreement and keep your promises and further do not do

anything to jeopardize the terms of our Operator's Agreement or Mutual Release Agreement dated March 7, 1962, I will cancel the Operator's Agreement. I also further refuse to renew your lease which expires April 29th, 1964. This attitude on my part is substantiated by your vicious letters of July 28th and August 20th, 1962."

Subsequently, under date of September 15, 1962, plaintiff notified Tastee-Freez that its "notice of refusal to renew my lease in March 1964, with one year of the operator's agreement and the conditional sale contract still to run, is a prima facie anticipatory breach of contract, and I have the legal right to choose to sue for retribution of damages immediately." Following this letter, plaintiff terminated his "Operator's Agreement" as of November 14, 1962.

Plaintiff, proceeding pro se, filed a 4-count complaint, to which was attached copies of the agreements and pertinent correspondence. The defendants named were: (1) Chicago Tastee-Freez Corporation; (2) Alvin D. Rose; (3) Allied Business Credit Corporation; (4) Harlee Manufacturing Company; and (5) Freez-King Corporation. This complaint was stricken on January 24, 1963. An amended complaint was filed February 25, 1963, and was stricken June 17, 1963. Plaintiff's second amended complaint was filed August 6, 1963, and was stricken November 14, 1963.

Subsequently, the record indicates, the defendants, Allied Business Credit Corporation, Harlee Manufacturing Company, and Freez-King Corporation, filed petitions under Chapter XI of the Bankruptcy Act. Orders were entered in the United States District Court "continuing debtor as debtor in possession with authority to operate its business," and all claimants were "restrained and enjoined until further order of the Court from commencing or continuing any action

at law or suit in equity * * * against said debtor, or the debtor in possession, or any of its property * * *."

On November 15, 1963, plaintiff filed his third amended complaint, consisting of three counts. Count I alleges "[t]hat Allied Business Credit Corporation participated as finance company for three of the conditional sales contracts; to-wit: The purchase of and payment for three (3) Tastee-Freez truck (mobile) dispensing units." It alleges that Allied Business Credit Corporation refuses to remit an acknowledged credit balance in favor of plaintiff of $1,702.74. Count I prays for judgment in this amount, plus interest and costs "against Allied Business Credit Corporation, or Alvin D. Rose, or both jointly, plus punitive damages against both parties, jointly and severally, in the amount of $3,400.00. (Except as restrained by Federal Court order * * *)."

In Count II, plaintiff seeks to recover $500, plus interest, plus exemplary damages for fraud and deceit, from defendant Alvin D. Rose, because Rose made misrepresentations as to credits due plaintiff in a previous transaction between plaintiff and Rose, involving an unsuccessful venture with a Chicago Heights store and three "Tastee-Freez mobile units" (1-ton trucks). In Count III, plaintiff seeks damages from "Chicago Tastee-Freez Corporation and Alvin D. Rose." They, "on or about August 29, 1962, positively and without reservation, did repudiate the Operator's Agreement and the Conditional Sale Contract by the convenient contrivance of announcing a premature termination of the lease of the premises to be effective on April 29, 1964," because of which "plaintiff was caused to cease further operations at once for the reason that waiting the year, until the announced termination date, would only result in unnecessary heavy expenditures without benefit therefrom."

On February 18, 1964, the trial court continued generally all of the proceedings under Count I, pending the disposition of the proceedings in the United States District Court.

On May 7, 1964, an order was entered by the trial court, which struck Counts II and III of the amended complaint, and further ordered that "Chicago Tastee-Freez Corporation and Alvin D. Rose are hereby dismissed as parties defendant herein, with prejudice." This is the order from which plaintiff appeals.

Defendants contend that the order from which plaintiff "seeks to appeal, is not a final appealable order, judgment or decree within the meaning of Sec. 50(2) of the Illinois Civil Practice Act, Ill. Rev. Stat. (1963), Ch. 110, Sec. 50(2)." Defendants argue that there is no express finding in the order "that there is no just reason for delaying enforcement or appeal," and as the order adjudicates fewer than all of the claims involved in the action, the appeal should be dismissed. Cited is Ariola v. Nigro, 13 Ill.2d 200, 148 N.E.2d 787 (1958).

The Federal Court order restrained the plaintiff and other claimants from continuing the prosecution of his claim against Allied Business Credit Corporation "until further order of the Court." The trial court here "ordered that all proceedings upon Count I of the said Third Amended Complaint be and they are hereby continued generally * * * all pending the disposition of proceedings presently pending in the United States District Court for the Northern District of Illinois * * * or until the restraining orders entered in said proceedings shall have been vacated or modified * * *." [Emphasis supplied.] In his third amended complaint, plaintiff recognized that, pursuant to the Federal Court order, Allied Business Credit Corporation "is suspended as defendant herein until otherwise

ordered by said United States District Court * * *."

Count I of the third amended complaint remains to be disposed of by the trial court. Allied Business Credit Corporation, although in bankruptcy proceedings, is still a party defendant in this action, and has not been dismissed as a party defendant by any order of the trial court.

Multiple parties and multiple claims for relief, therefore, are involved in this action. The decree of the trial court appealed from, dismissing defendants Rose and Tastee-Freez and dismissing Counts II and III of the third amended complaint, "adjudicates fewer than all the claims or the rights and liabilities of fewer than all the parties." The trial court did not make an express finding "that there is no just reason for delaying enforcement or appeal." Under these circumstances, we hold section 50(2) of the Civil Practice Act does apply, and the order of May 7, 1964, is not appealable. (Ariola v. Nigro, 13 Ill.2d 200.) As was said in the Ariola case, at page 207:

> "[S]ection 50(2) was aimed at discouraging piecemeal appeals, in the absence of just reason, and at removing the uncertainty which existed when a final judgment was entered on less than all of the matters of controversy. * * * [It] fixes the procedure in the trial court as to the conditions affecting the terms upon which an appeal may be taken in advance of a determination of the entire case."

See, also, Weidler v. Westinghouse Elec. Corp., 37 Ill. App.2d 95, 98, 185 N.E.2d 100 (1962); and Simon v. Simon, 37 Ill. App.2d 100, 104, 185 N.E.2d 111 (1962).

For the reasons stated, the present appeal is dismissed.

APPEAL DISMISSED.

BURMAN, P.J., and KLUCZYNSKI, J., concur.

ABSTRACT ONLY.

STATE OF ILLINOIS

APPELLATE COURT

FOURTH DISTRICT

General No. M-10617 | Agenda No. 1

People of the State of Illinois, Plaintiff-Appellee	
vs.	
Glenn E. Pierceson, Defendant-Appellant	Appeal from Circuit Court Sangamon County

CRAVEN, J.:

This appeal was brought from a judgment and conviction in the Magistrate's Division of the Circuit Court of Sangamon County, Illinois, entered on July 27, 1964. The defendant was found guilty of improper lane usage, in violation of sec. 60 (a) of the Uniform Act Regulating Traffic on Highways, and fined $10.00 and costs.

On April 17, 1964, the defendant, Glenn E. Pierceson, was driving a tractor-trailer truck north on U. S. Route 66, a four-lane highway, approaching Springfield from the south. The place of the alleged offense is located approximately two miles south of Springfield, and the defendant was driving his truck occupying the outer or right-hand lane of traffic. To the right of the outer or right-hand lane of traffic a convertible automobile had pulled off to the side of the highway and the door on the driver's side opened extending to the edge of the pavement. As the defendant approached the parked automobile he partially moved his truck into the left or passing lane of traffic. The evidence is disputant as to whether or not the defendant made use of his turn signals before he moved into the left or passing lane.

The defendant was followed for some distance by two automobiles which had been overtaking him in the left or passing lane. The second of these automobiles

was a marked State police car driven by Trooper John J. Greenan. The defendant's movement into the left or passing lane caused these two drivers to apply their brakes and slow their vehicles 10 to 15 miles per hour.

The defendant then returned to his lane of traffic and was later stopped and issued a citation for improper lane usage. Trooper Greenan was unaware of the stopped convertible on the shoulder of the highway at the time of the defendant's movement into the passing lane; however, he did acknowledge that the presence of the automobile was brought to his attention by the defendant at the time he issued the citation.

The statute under which the defendant was charged and convicted states:

> "Whenever any roadway has been divided into 2 or more clearly marked lanes for traffic the following rules in addition to all others consistent herewith shall apply.
>
> "(a) A vehicle shall be driven as nearly as practicable entirely within a single lane and shall not be moved from

such lane until the driver has first ascertained that such movement can be made with safety."

. . . . . .

Ill. Rev. Stat. 1963, ch. $95^{1}/_{2}$, par. 157, sec. 60(a).

Under the above statute the State has the burden of establishing beyond a reasonable doubt that the defendant moved from one lane of traffic to another, and also that he made such movement without ascertaining that it could be done with safety. There is no dispute to the fact that the defendant at least partially moved his slower vehicle into the passing lane of traffic. The issue presented is whether the defendant ascertained that such movement could be made with safety.

The State contends that the evidence is sufficient to establish that element beyond a reasonable doubt. The State argues that the defendant's movement into the passing lane was made for no apparent reason and that

safety considerations for the people in the stopped automobile were remote and conjectural. It is true that the movement into the passing lane was for no apparent reason to the State trooper. However, the trooper was unaware of the automobile on the shoulder of the highway until it was pointed out to him by the defendant after he was stopped and being issued a citation. The State trooper further testified that in his opinion this movement constituted a hazard.

Certainly, in varying degrees, any interchange of traffic on a busy highway constitutes a hazard or risk. The question under this statute is whether this movement was a calculated action in light of existing traffic conditions or whether it was a careless and blind act oblivious to the safety of others on the highway. All motorists are required to drive in one lane of traffic "as nearly as practicable." This is not an inflexible or unyielding rule. It is tempered with practicality and reason in the use of lanes of traffic in light of existing conditions.

Although there is a dispute as to the proximity of the passing automobiles when the movement was made, and also as to whether the defendant made use of his turn signals, we must assume that the trial court resolved these factual issues adversely to the defendant. Even conceding these factual issues, there still is a lack of positive evidence which would support a finding that under the admitted traffic conditions the defendant was guilty of improper lane usage.

The evidence is undisputed that the defendant left his lane of traffic for a specific reason and that he was aware of the automobiles approaching from the rear in the passing lane. The evidence is also undisputed that the defendant did safely move from his lane of traffic into the passing lane. The fact that this maneuver caused the passing vehicles to decrease their speed 10 or 15 miles per hour by applying their brakes does not establish that the defendant made such movement without first ascertaining

whether it could be done safely in light of existing conditions. Finally, it is undisputed that the trooper was unaware of the traffic condition which in the defendant's judgment necessitated the movement.

The state of a man's mind is never the subject of direct proof; however, there are no facts here to justify even a circumstantial inference that the defendant failed to ascertain the safety of the movement which he made. In light of this record, the defendant was the only person aware of all the factors necessary to exercise a split-second determination as to what was "practicable" and "safe" in light of the situation which confronted him. Certainly, his move was more judicious than to crowd the stopped automobile and possibly be confronted with the alternative of a collision with an unwary occupant or suddenly swerving directly into the path of passing traffic.

We find the evidence, viewed in a light most favorable to the prosecution, to be totally insufficient to establish the defendant's guilt beyond a

reasonable doubt, and therefore reverse the judgment and conviction of the Magistrate's Division, Circuit Court, Sangamon County.

Reversed

SMITH, P.J. and TRAPP, J., concur.

APPELLATE COURT OF ILLINOIS

SECOND DISTRICT

THE DEPARTMENT OF PUBLIC WORKS & BUILDINGS OF THE STATE OF ILLINOIS, Plaintiff-Appellee,	)	Appeal from the Circuit Court of Lake County, Illinois
vs.	)	
ROY J. SMITH, Successor Trustee, et al, Defendant-Appellant.	)	

ABRAHAMSON, P. J.

This proceeding was originally filed in the County Court of Lake County, which court is now a part of the circuit Court of Lake County. The proceeding was brought to acquire 5 parcels of land for highway purposes. Defendants filed a motion to traverse and dismiss. After lengthy hearings, the trial court denied the traverse and entered orders permitting a "quick take" by the Petitioner. Subsequently, a jury trial was held on the issue of compensation and the total verdict was in the amount of $2,000.00.

Defendants appealed and stated their theory of the case as follows:

"The respondent-appellants' theory of the case is that the Petitioner attacked the title and ownership of the Respondents' land being taken in the presence of the condemnation jury; the petitioner claimed title and ownership to a 80 foot highway prior to the filing of the petition to con-

demn; the petitioner claimed title to Belvidere Road under the doctrine of adverse user before and to a condemnation jury; the petitioner improperly described the area needed for road purposes in its petition to condemn; the petitioner improperly applied the market value rule to property which the petitioner characterized as having a special or particular use; and the Trial Court improperly struck the Cross-Petition; and the Attorney for the Condemnor presented prejudicial motions and prejudicial and improper arguments to the jury so that the verdicts rendered and the judgments entered thereon do not award to the Respondents the just compensation which the law requires."

Belvidere Road is an existing State Highway which runs Westerly from Waukegan in Lake County, Illinois. On or about May 1, 1958, Petitioner instituted condemnation proceedings in which Petitioner claimed a 30 foot easement and right of way for highway purposes on either side of the center line of Belvidere Road and sought to acquire an additional 10 feet on either side of Belvidere Road, increasing the overall right of way from 60 to 80 feet with the intention of replacing the two lane highway then existing along Belvidere Road with a four lane highway. The defendants are the owners of three parcels of land lying to the South of Belvidere Road and two parcels lying to the North.

At the hearing on the traverse, defendants contended that they owned fee simple, absolute title, to the center line of existing Belvidere Road, that the legal description of the taking should run to the center line without exception, and that compensation should be adjudicated accordingly. The

trial court overruled the traverse, holding that petitioner had a right of way by prescription to sixty feet, (30 feet each side of the center line). Thereupon, a quick take order was entered adjudicating preliminary just compensation, the funds were deposited, an order vesting title was entered, and the defendants thereafter withdrew the deposit of $6,044.71.

Later, the defendants filed a cross-petition which then admitted that the petitioner had a right of way over sixteen feet on each side of the center line, and averred that defendants owned the next fourteen feet on each side of the center line and that petitioner sought to condemn and pay for only the outer ten feet on each side of the center line. Defendants prayed for damages to the two fourteen foot strips on each side of the road adjacent to and beyond each parcel of the admitted sixteen foot right of way on each side of the centerline of Belvidere Road. They also sought compensation for the taking of the ten foot parcels on each side of the road and damage to the remainder generally.

No draft order had been entered formalizing the Court's ruling as to the existing right of way at the conclusion of the traverse hearing. Because of the absence of a formal court order spelling out the Court's finding that the petitioner had an easement by prescription over sixty feet (30 feet each side of the center line), and upon the insistence of the defendants that this issue be relitigated and complete proofs required, the court ruled that it would "reconsider the question of whether an easement was or

was not established and require proofs to be submitted in the present trial on the question as to whether or not there was a thirty foot easement (on each side of the center line) established by the State." Petitioner suggested that evidence on that issue be taken outside the presence of the jury, but defendants did not join in this request. Adequate testimony was presented before the jury to establish that the Condemnor had an easement by prescription over sixty feet. The trial court then struck the cross-petition as to the fourteen feet on the basis of the evidence and precluded any defense testimony as to the damage thereto.

Defendants, for their first two contentions, argue that the court erred in permitting petitioner to introduce evidence attacking defendants' title to the various strips of land involved. Defendants correctly state that the law is that in condemnation cases the jury is impanalled merely to ascertain and determine the just compensation to be awarded to the owners of the property being taken or damaged and that no issue of ownership or title can be presented to the jury. The question of title, if any, is preliminary to the submission of the question of damages to the jury and must be determined before the jury is impanelled. Metropolitan El. Ry. Co. v. Eschner, 232 Ill. 210; Chic. and Mil. Elec. Ry. Co. v. Diver, 213 Ill. 26.

The defendants contend that the Court erred in striking the counter-petition as to their ownership of the fourteen foot strips described in said petition and complain that evidence on this issue was presented to the jury. It is clear from the record in this case that before submitting the case to the jury the Court

struck the counter-petition as to the fourteen feet and no evidence of title was submitted to the jury. That plaintiffs had a pre-existing right of way over these fourteen foot strips was properly determined by the Court. City of Highland Park v. Driscoll, 24 Ill. 2d 281.

Petitioner never questioned that defendants owned fee simple, absolute title to the center line of Belvidere Road as it existed as of date of the filing of these proceedings, but claimed an easement for highway purposes. The question of the easement was not submitted to the jury for determination. The trial judge in dismissing the cross-petition as to the fourteen foot strips made this determination. Although the propriety of this procedure may be questioned, the failure of the defendants to join in the petitioners' request that the matter be heard outside the presence of the jury leads us to conclude that this was not prejudicial. However, if we view such procedure as prejudicial error, even then such error was induced by defendants and they cannot complain because of it. City of Waukegan v. Stanczak, 6 Ill. 2d 594, 608.

The court did not err in striking the cross-petition. Defendants contend that the taking of the additional ten foot strip beyond the fourteen foot strip described in the cross-petition is tantamount to the taking of the fourteen foot strips. The court properly determined that the fourteen foot strips had been subject to an easement for highway purposes by prescription for years and the proofs so disclosed that the taking of the additional ten foot strips for highway purposes expanded the highway and in no way

affected the interest of the defendants in the property described in the cross-petition. City of Highland Park v. Driscoll, supra.

Error is urged in the admission of a County zoning ordinance requiring that all subdivisions adjoining State roads shall provide for a minimum width of not less than one hundred feet, for highway purposes. The property adjoining had not been subdivided and was for the most part vacant and unimproved. Petitioners' proof indicated the highest and best use of the premises was for a residential subdivision. It appears that the ordinance relates to and is pertinent to this issue and was properly admitted. City of Chicago v. Pridmore, 12 Ill. 2d 447, 451.

Defendants argue that the landscape or planter easement placed the premises in a "special use" catagory and, therefore, the market value test should not apply. Defendants failed to offer any proof of value predicated on a "special use" theory nor does there appear any reason to conclude that merely because of the existence of the planter easement a special use is created. Peo. Gas Light & Coke Co. v. Buckles, 24 Ill. 2d 520, 531 and 532. Generally exceptions occur only when property has special capabilities which make it unmarketable at its true value due to unique improvements, such as a church, a school or a railroad terminal. Housing Authority v. Kosydor, 17 Ill. 2d 602, 605 and 606.

Defendants also contend that counsel for the petitioner was guilty of improper and prejudicial conduct during the trial and that his arguments at the close were inflammatory and prejudicial.

Defendants contend it was prejudicial for petitioner's counsel, on cross examination, to ask one of the defendants how long he had been a land speculator. This was permissive in that defendant testified in direct examination in response to questions from his counsel as follows:

> "Q. In your business as a real estate broker, do you buy and sell land?
>
> A. Yes. We have been buying and selling land for our investors and for our own speculative account for well over twenty years, in fact, some of it for almost forty years."

Defendants also object that petitioner's attorney charged one of the defendants and the attorney for the other defendants with being in contempt in connection with certain testimony that the defendant in question had given. The record indicates that on the occasion in question the defendant and his attorney persisted in seeking to introduce evidence to which the trial court had sustained objections and because of the persistence of the defendant and his attorney in this matter we deem it not prejudicial for petitioner's attorney to charge the attorney or the defendant with being in contempt.

Defendant also states that the petitioner attempted to show negiotiations toward a settlement of this matter. The record fails to show any reference to negiotiations and we find no prejudice to the defendant on this ground.

We have read the closing arguments of counsel for petitioner and do not find as contended by defendants, that petitioner's arguments were in any way inflammatory or prejudicial.

Finally, the record discloses that the jury verdict was well within the range of the testimony presented. The Illinois Courts

on review have refused to disturb the verdict of the jury in condemnation cases, despite some irregularities in proceedings. Here the jury has viewed the premises and no prejudice or clear and palpable mistake is shown. Dept. of Public Works v. Drobnick, 14 Ill. 2d 28; Dept. Public Works & Bldg. v. Bloomer, 28 Ill. 2d 267.

For the reasons above stated the decision of the lower court is affirmed.

JUDGMENT AFFIRMED.

MORAN, J. and DAVIS, J. concur.

49560

(61 I.A.2d 325)

GEORGE J. FRANKS,

Plaintiff-Appellant,

v.

PAUL SHEMNECK, OLGA JEUK, JACOB JEUK, and MARGE MALMIN (also known as Margaret Malmin),

Defendants,

PAUL SHEMNECK and MARGE MALMIN,

Appellees.

APPEAL FROM THE FIRST MUNICIPAL DISTRICT, CIRCUIT COURT OF COOK COUNTY

MR. JUSTICE LYONS DELIVERED THE OPINION OF THE COURT:

This is an appeal from an order of judgment entered in favor of Defendants-Appellees, Paul Shemneck and Marge Malmin.

Plaintiff brought a joint forcible detainer action for possession of an apartment and recovery of a $600 rent arrearage accumulated over a six month period beginning February, 1962. Judgment was entered against defendants, Jacob and Olga Jeuk. Thereafter an alias claim was filed against defendants, Malmin and Shemneck. Malmin filed her appearance by counsel. Shemneck filed his appearance pro se. Malmin filed her answer denying she was indebted to plaintiff. She admitted she resided with her mother and father, Jacob and Olga Jeuk, in the subject premises, but stated she did so solely as a child living with a parent. Shemneck failed to answer.

On October 8, 1963, plaintiff filed a written motion asking for judgment against Shemneck for failing to answer and against Malmin based on her answer. The written motion contained an affidavit executed by plaintiff which stated: that Malmin had resided in the premises for several years, including the six month period involved; that she is a daughter of the Jeuks; that she is of legal age; that periodically, while occupying the premises in question, she would bring her son to live with her; that she had not paid any rent for the months sued for; and that she admitted living in the premises, but denied she is liable for rent on the ground that she resided there solely as a child living with a

parent. On October 8, an order of default was entered against Shemneck. Trial was set for November 19, 1963 as to Malmin.

Immediately prior to the trial an order was entered which referred to the judgment entered against Shemneck on October 8, 1963 and further stated: that said judgment was improperly entered by the court; that therefore it is vacated and set aside, and cause set for trial on November 19, 1963; and that Bernard Kurlan is appointed by the court as attorney for Shemneck.

At the trial Malmin testified, pursuant to Section 60 of the Civil Practice Act, that defendants Jacob and Olga Jeuk were the original tenants; that she was not a party to the original month to month leasing; that the Jeuks had resided there several years prior to the initiation of these proceedings; that defendant, Shemneck, is her uncle; and that both her uncle and herself had resided with the Jeuks in the same apartment, paying them for room and board.

Defendant, Shemneck, was present in court and was also called to testify pursuant to Section 60 of the Civil Practice Act. He testified that he lived with the Jeuks and paid them room and board.

It is plaintiff's theory of the case that defendants, Malmin and Shemneck, owe plaintiff rent in that they occupied the apartment leased to Jacob and Olga Jeuk. Chapter 80, paragraph 1 of the Illinois Revised Statutes (1963) states as follows:

> That the owners of lands, his executors or administrators, may sue for and recover rent therefor, or a fair and reasonable satisfaction for the use and occupation thereof, by a civil action, in any court of competent jurisdiction, in any of the following cases: ... Second: When lands are held and occupied by any person without any special agreement for rent....

Plaintiff first contends that defendants Malmin and Shemneck are liable to plaintiff for the $600 owed by Olga and Jacob Jeuk to plaintiff because said defendants occupied the apartment leased to the Jeuks. Plaintiff reasons that, because of the above statute, any person occupying premises without any special agreement for rent becomes liable

to the landlord if the rent is not paid by the tenant. It is plaintiff's position that no special agreement for rent existed between plaintiff and defendants Malmin and Shemneck and thus they fall within the purview of the statute.

[1-3] We hold that Malmin and Shemneck are not liable as an agreement for rent existed between plaintiff and the Jeuks. We disagree with plaintiff's contention that the Act applies to any person occupying the property. An examination of the cases cited by plaintiff reveals that they primarily embrace those situations where the person occupying the improved or unimproved land of another is a trespasser. Cullet v. Rosenberg, 306 Ill. App. 267, 28 N.E.2d 351 (1940). Cauley v. Northern Trust, 315 Ill. App. 307, 43 N.E.2d 147 (1942). Under these circumstances the law implies both the creation of a tenancy and liability for reasonable rent on the occupiers of the premises by establishing privity of contract between the owners of the land and the occupiers. Privity of estate exists so long as the occupier is allowed to remain on the premises. An action for use and occupation will not lie where there is no privity between the plaintiff and the person in possession. Fender v. Rogers, 97 Ill. App. 280 (1901). In the instant case there is no privity of contract or estate between plaintiff and defendants Malmin and Shemneck. Defendants are not trespassers as they occupy the land through the lessees as licensees or boarders; thus no tenancy can be implied.

Any other interpretation of the statute would be grossly inequitable to persons standing in a position similar to that of defendants Malmin and Shemneck. These defendants have paid room and board to lessees Jacob and Olga Jeuk and would again be subjected to the payment of rent if we were to hold them liable.

Furthermore, the record indicates that Malmin and Shemneck are closely related to the lessees and have a right to occupy the premises with the permission of the lessees. Plaintiff's contention that a lessee has no right to bring in boarders when no restriction appears in the

lease does not have to be further answered in this decision.

Plaintiff's second contention is that the default judgment entered on October 8, 1963, against Shemneck was improperly set aside, because Section 72 of the Civil Practice Act requires that a written petition be filed with the court. We disagree with plaintiff's contention for a number of reasons.

The first reason is that plaintiff is raising this objection for the first time on appeal. Plaintiff is estopped from bringing up this objection as it was not made at the trial.

The second reason is that the parties stipulated to the facts of the case in lieu of a transcript of proceedings. Plaintiff stipulated to the vacation of the order of default and is estopped from denying its validity as no objection is found in the stipulated transcription of proceeding.

Finally, defendants Malmin and Shemneck were called under Chapter 60 of the Civil Practice Act as adverse witnesses. The action of plaintiff in calling Malmin and Shemneck as adverse witnesses further estops him from raising the objection that a written petition was not filed with the court. Plaintiff contends, however, that Shemneck was called as a witness only in the Malmin proceedings. We disagree with this contention. In order for Shemneck to be called as an adverse witness he would have to be an adverse party. We presume that Shemneck was called by plaintiff to testify against Shemneck's own interests. Plaintiff is estopped from asserting Shemneck's failure to file written pleadings by calling Shemneck as an adverse witness.

It is true, as plaintiff contends, that Shemneck was represented by court appointed counsel and that it would have been a simple matter for counsel to have filed written pleadings. As pointed out above, however, plaintiff failed to make the necessary objections. For the above reasons the judgment is affirmed.

JUDGMENT AFFIRMED.

BURKE, P.J., and BRYANT, J., concur.

49722

31 I.A.2 326

PEOPLE OF THE STATE OF ILLINOIS, Plaintiff-Appellee, v. JAMES EZELL, Defendant-Appellant.	)	APPEAL FROM CIRCUIT COURT COUNTY DEPARTMENT CRIMINAL DIVISION COOK COUNTY

MR. PRESIDING JUSTICE BURKE DELIVERED THE OPINION OF THE COURT:

Defendant was found guilty at a bench trial of unlawful possession of narcotics and sentenced from two to three years in the penitentiary. He appeals.

A pre-trial motion to suppress evidence was filed by defendant pursuant to Section 114-12 of the Code of Criminal Procedure of 1963. Ill. Rev. Stat. 1963, Chap. 38, Par. 114-12. At the hearing on the motion defendant testified that, about 2:30 A.M. on April 3, 1963, he left a friend's home on the south side of Chicago after watching television and drove to a nearby tavern for some orange juice to relieve a headache. He parked his automobile a short distance from the tavern and was walking toward the tavern when he was stopped by two police officers of the Chicago Police Department, Narcotics Unit, one of whom was an acquaintance of defendant. One of the officers said to defendant, "I heard you was doing wrong," which defendant stated he denied. The officer then asked defendant what he had in his pocket, to which defendant replied, "Nothing." The officer put his hand into defendant's right-hand pants pocket and removed a packet of narcotics, which is the subject of this action. Defendant was placed under arrest and taken to police headquarters where more narcotics were found on his person. Defendant testified that at the time of the arrest he was doing nothing wrong, but simply walking on the public street toward the tavern. No warrant had been issued for either defendant's arrest or the search of his person. Neither of the arresting officers was called as a witness at the hearing

on the motion.

The motion to suppress challenged the legality of the search and seizure made in connection with the arrest on the ground that the arrest was unlawful. The trial court denied the motion for the reason that defendant failed to produce evidence that the officers had no reasonable grounds upon which to effect the arrest. It was the opinion of the court that, in order to sustain the allegations contained in the motion, it was incumbent upon defendant to call the officers as witnesses to prove that they did not make the arrest based upon a past criminal offense which they had reasonable grounds to believe defendant committed.

A trial was had and defendant was convicted solely upon the testimony of one of the arresting officers and the narcotics taken from his person at the time of the arrest and that taken later at police headquarters.

Defendant contends the evidence brought out at the hearing on the motion to suppress established that his arrest was unlawful and that therefore the search and seizure made in connection therewith were unlawful. The State maintains the defendant did not sustain the burden of showing the officers had no reasonable grounds upon which to effect the arrest since no evidence was presented showing that the officers did not make the arrest based upon a past offense and a reasonable belief that defendant committed it. The State's position is predicated on the fact that the statute places the burden upon the defendant to show the search and seizure to be unlawful, rather than upon the State to show them to be lawful.

Section 114-12 of the Code of Criminal Procedure of 1963 states in part:

> "(b)...The judge shall receive evidence of any issue of fact necessary to determine the motion and the burden of proving that the search and seizure were unlawful shall be on the defendant...." (Ill. Rev. Stat. 1963, Chap. 38, Par.114-12.)

Whether the search and seizure were lawful or unlawful in the instant case depends upon whether the officers effected a lawful arrest.

On the date of defendant's arrest, arrests without warrants were governed by Ill. Rev. Stat. 1961, Chap. 38, Pars. 22-25 and 657. Paragraph 22-25 deals with arrests made in connection with violations of the Uniform Narcotic Drug Act, and provides that officers and employees of the Division of Narcotic Control, and other law enforcement officers whose duties are to enforce the Act, may arrest without a warrant for violations of the Act committed in their presence or where the person making the arrest has reasonable grounds to believe that the person to be arrested is committing or has committed a violation. Paragraph 657, which was subsequently repealed, dealt in general with arrests made without warrants, and provided that a peace officer could arrest for offenses in his presence or when an offense had in fact been committed and the officer had reasonable grounds for believing that the person to be arrested committed it. While the requirements of Paragraph 657 were more restrictive, requiring a criminal offense to have in fact been committed before the arresting officer could effect an arrest where an offense was not openly committed in his presence, both provisions required that the arresting officer have reasonable grounds in believing that the person to be arrested committed an offense, or, in the case of an arrest for the violation of the Uniform Narcotic Drug Act, reasonable grounds in believing that an offense was then being committed.

Lawful search and seizure may be effected in connection with a lawful arrest made without a warrant. People v. Pitts, 26 Ill.2d 395. If an arrest is unlawful, having been made without reasonable grounds, evidence of a crime discovered in a subsequent search cannot relate back to justify the arrest. People v. Galloway, 7 Ill.2d 527. What

constitutes "reasonable grounds" depends upon the factual and practical considerations of everyday life upon which reasonable and prudent men, and not legal technicians, act. People v. Pitts, 26 Ill.2d 395. It is undisputed in the instant case that the officers had no warrant for defendant's arrest; it is also undisputed that, at the time of the arrest, defendant was not engaged in the open commission of a criminal offense. Defendant's testimony was the only evidence adduced at the hearing on the motion to suppress; consequently, the only question for determination here is whether defendant made out a _prima facie_ case that his arrest was made without reasonable cause. We are of the opinion that a _prima facie_ case was made out showing the arrest to have been made without reasonable grounds and that the resulting search and seizure were consequently unlawful.

Defendant's uncontroverted evidence shows that the arresting officers had no warrant for either his arrest or the search of his person. At the time of the arrest he was doing nothing more than walking on a public street. When the police officer commented to defendant that he heard defendant was doing wrong, defendant denied doing anything wrong. After asking defendant what he had in his pocket, to which defendant replied "nothing," the officer searched defendant, seized the narcotics used as evidence against him at trial and placed him under arrest. On these facts defendant made out a _prima facie_ case for the unlawfulness of the search and seizure by reason of an unlawful arrest. See People v. Thomas, 25 Ill.2d 559; People v. Roebuck, 25 Ill.2d 108; People v. McDonald, 51 Ill. App.2d 316. To hold that Section 114-12 required defendant to go further in making out a _prima facie_ case, relative to producing evidence that he had committed no offense in the past, would be to place an impossible burden upon him, namely, requiring him to account for all his past activities for an indefinite period of time to show he had done nothing in the past upon which the arrest could

have been predicated. Defendant initially sustained his burden on this point when he testified that he denied doing anything wrong in response to the statement made by the police officer at the time of the arrest. The burden was then upon the State to come forward with evidence to show why defendant was arrested. Defendant was not required to call the arresting officers as witnesses to establish that they had no reasonable grounds to believe defendant was then engaged in the commission of or had committed an offense upon which an arrest could have been predicated. This is not to say that the State has the burden of proving the search and seizure to be lawful, but merely the burden of going forward with evidence to negate the _prima facie_ case made out by defendant that the search and seizure were unlawful by reason of an unlawful arrest.

There being nothing in the record to rebut defendant's evidence, the motion to suppress should have been sustained and the narcotics seized from defendant should not have been used against him at trial.

The judgment is reversed.

JUDGMENT REVERSED.

BRYANT, J., and LYONS, J., concur.

49989

(61 I.A.2 342)

TALBOT MILLS, INC., a corporation,
Plaintiff-Appellant,

v.

SAM BENEZRA and MORRIS BENEZRA, individually and as co-partners doing business as SUPER TOGS CO.,
Defendants-Appellees,

and

GOLDBLATT BROS., INC., a corporation,
Garnishee-Defendant-Appellee.

APPEAL FROM THE CIRCUIT COURT OF COOK COUNTY FIRST MUNICIPAL DISTRICT.

MR. JUSTICE DRUCKER DELIVERED THE OPINION OF THE COURT.

Plaintiff appeals from a summary judgment in favor of defendants Sam and Morris Benezra. A writ of attachment was issued based on a claim for the purchase price of goods sold to defendants by plaintiff. The statement of claim designated defendants as Sam and Morris Benezra doing business as Super Togs Co. and doing business as Super Togs, Inc. Defendants Sam and Morris Benezra, individually amd as co-partners doing business as Super Togs Co., moved for summary judgment. The affidavit of Sam Benezra on which the summary judgment is predicated stated that Super Togs, Inc. was an active, existing corporation and that "all orders for merchandise, which are the subject matter of the within suit, were placed by said Super Togs, Inc...."

In Tansey v. Robinson, 24 Ill. App. 2d 227, at 237, the court said that "movant's affidavit will be strictly construed and must leave no question of defendant's right to judgment...."

Since Sam Benezra's affidavit states no evidentiary facts concerning the placement of the orders, his conclusion that the orders were placed by the corporation does not establish a right to summary judgment.

The court struck the affidavit of plaintiff's salesman, Theodore S. Greene, which stated with particularity the circumstances surrounding the taking of the original order from Sam Benezra in the name of

Super Togs Co. and the reasons for subsequent entries in the name of the corporation. On Defendants' Exhibit 1 (the first order) the word "Inc." was stricken and Defendants' Exhibit 2 had an illegible signature but no corporate designation for "Buyer." Other exhibits show confirmations of orders by plaintiff seller but no writing signed by the buyer. In view of these facts, the counter-affidavit of Greene should not have been stricken as being self-serving and contradictory to the exhibits.

It therefore appears that there is a genuine issue of fact as to whether the goods were ordered by Sam Benezra as a partner of Super Togs Co. or as an officer of Super Togs, Inc.

The court denied plaintiff's motion for the production of the account books of Super Togs, Inc., noting that the corporation was not a party to the suit. Rule 17 of the Supreme Court (Ill. Rev. Stat., 1963, ch. 110, § 101.17) provides that not only a party but any other person may be ordered "to produce specified documents, relating to the merits of the matter in litigation...."

The court also curtailed discovery by plaintiff of information which was relevant to the issue of the identity of the buyer. Full discovery should have been permitted in accordance with the rules. Zemel v. Chateau Royale Corp., 35 Ill. App. 2d 313.

We cite with approval from a statement in Midwest Grocery Co. v. Danno, 29 Ill. App. 2d 118, at page 123:

> "The purpose of the summary judgment procedure is not to try an issue of fact, but rather to determine whether there is an issue of fact. The matter is necessarily inquisitorial. If there is a material issue of fact, it must be submitted to the jury. The right of the moving party to a judgment should be free from doubt." (Citing cases.)

The judgment is reversed and the cause is remanded for such other and further proceedings as are not inconsistent with the views herein expressed.

Judgment reversed and cause remanded.

REVERSED AND REMANDED.

McCormick, P.J., and English, J., concur.
Publish Abstract Only.

50249

WIEBOLDT STORES, INC., Plaintiff-Appellee, v. EMILIE MAUTNER a/k/a EMILIE N. WANDERER and ERWIN W. MAUTNER, On Appeal of EMILIE MAUTNER a/k/a EMILIE N. WANDERER, Defendant-Appellant.	)	61 I.A.2 368 APPEAL FROM THE MUNICIPAL COURT OF CHICAGO.

MR. PRESIDING JUSTICE DEMPSEY DELIVERED THE OPINION OF THE COURT.

The defendant, a married woman who was separated from her husband, purchased some articles, which are described as "necessaries," at the plaintiff's store and charged them to her husband's account. The plaintiff sued the defendant and upon her motion her husband was joined as a party-defendant. A settlement was made with the husband and the case against him was dismissed. A judgment of $79.78 was recovered against the defendant. A decree for separate maintenance was subsequently entered in her favor.

She has appealed on the principal ground that her husband was responsible for her support and for the merchandise purchased by her prior to their legal separation.

The plaintiff-appellee filed no appearance in this court and has filed no brief. Because of the failure to file a brief, as provided by Appellate Court rule 5(2)(k) it is unnecessary to review this case further. 541 Briar Place v. Harman, 46 Ill. App. 2d 1, 196 N.E.2d 498; Wright v. C.T.A., 43 Ill. App. 2d 408, 193 N.E.2d 597.

The judgment is reversed.

Reversed.

Sullivan and Schwartz, JJ., concur.

Abstract only.

ABST.

49936

MICHAEL S. ACOSTA and BERNICE ACOSTA,	)	
Plaintiffs-Appellants,	)	APPEAL FROM
vs.	)	CIRCUIT COURT,
REGINALD J. HOLZER,	)	COOK COUNTY.
Defendant-Appellee.	)	

MR. JUSTICE MURPHY DELIVERED THE OPINION OF THE COURT.

This is a two count action at law, with jury demand, for fraud and deceit. After plaintiffs filed their second amended complaint, an order was entered sustaining a motion to strike and dismiss as to defendants Batey and Motion Picture Corporation of America. Subsequently, the trial court struck the second amended complaint as to the remaining defendant, Reginald Holzer, and dismissed the action, and it is from this order that plaintiffs appeal.

The issue on appeal is whether Count I of the second amended complaint states a cause of action at law in fraud and deceit against defendant Holzer.

Initially, we agree with defendant Holzer that although a motion to dismiss admits all facts well pleaded in the complaint, "the indispensable requirement of the complaint is that the allegations state a cause of action." Kita v. Y.M.C.A. of Metropolitan Chicago, 47 Ill. App.2d 409, 198 N.E.2d 174 (1964).

Also, a complaint grounded on fraud and deceit "'must plead sufficient acts or facts relied upon to establish the fraud' * * *; and that the facts alleged must be such as 'constitute fraud in themselves or are facts on which fraud will be necessarily implied.' * * * The elements of fraud, which must be pleaded, have been set forth in many cases. They are representation, falsity, scienter,

deception and injury * * *." Tate v. Jackson, 22 Ill. App.2d 471, 473, 161 N.E.2d 156 (1959).

In summary, Count I of the verified second amended complaint alleges that in the early part of 1961, plaintiffs were introduced to defendant Holzer, an attorney at law, by defendant William D. Batey, director and vice president of defendant Motion Picture Corporation of America, referred to as "MPCA." MPCA had been incorporated in Illinois in August, 1960, to produce and distribute "low-budget" feature length films, and Holzer was its president.

In March, 1961, Batey inquired of plaintiffs "if they would be interested in investing in defendant MPCA" and in "End Of Innocence," a partnership formed and organized by Holzer and Batey in December, 1960, "to raise funds to finance the production and distribution of films by MPCA." Holzer "worked assiduously to obtain the trust and confidence of the Acostas," urging them to "invest up to $10,000 in the venture." Plaintiffs declined to invest because all of their funds were tied up in an aviation venture. During the summer of 1961, the aviation venture collapsed, and plaintiffs, "on the basis of their trust and confidence in him as a result of the earlier conversations about investing in MPCA," retained Holzer as their attorney to salvage as much as possible.

Holzer spent some time on the matter and also organized a new corporation, Space Age, Inc., "in his capacity as attorney for the Acostas. Holzer refused to take a fee for his services, saying that he felt 'sorry' for the Acostas and that he hoped they would invest whatever might be recovered in MPCA." Nothing was recovered from the aviation venture, and on or about September 1, 1961, Holzer advised the Acostas that nothing further could be done.

Shortly after September 1, 1961, Holzer proposed that the

Acostas invest $50,000 in "MPCA" and "End Of Innocence," which would enable them "to recoup their losses in the aviation venture, and make 'bundles' more besides, for the venture was sure to be a success. The film to be produced would be a documentary of Communism. Holzer introduced the Acostas to other investors in the venture, who were identified as law clients of Holzer * * *. Holzer stated that he had investigated the matter exhaustively for two years; that he had important contacts in Hollywood including his brother * * *; and that 'important' people in Hollywood wanted a 'piece' of the picture." Plaintiffs told Holzer they had no available funds--"only debts from the aviation venture." Holzer then offered to arrange financing.

Because of their importance, the following allegations of Count I are quoted in detail.

"18. On or about September 16, 1961, at about 6:00 P.M., Holzer met with the Acostas at the Acostas' home in Kenosha County, Wisconsin. Holzer's wife was also present. Holzer said that he could obtain financing for the Acostas on the following terms:

> $50,000 for 1 year, with a 'commission' of $10,000, to be reduced to $6,000 if the loan were repaid in full in six months. Holzer personally guaranteed payment of any 'commission' owing in excess of $6,000. Loan to be secured by a second mortgage on the Acostas' home.

"19. At the same time and place, Holzer stated further that in order to 'make the loan possible', it would be necessary for the Acostas to incorporate their home and adjoining real estate in Kenosha County, Wisconsin; the loan would then be made in the name of the corporation. As their attorney, Holzer said he would organize the necessary corporation for the Acostas.

"20. At the same time and place, Holzer reiterated that large profits to the investors were a virtual certainty, and urged the Acostas in the strongest possible terms to invest on the basis outlined above. Plaintiff Bernice Acosta was impressed, but nevertheless expressed apprehension that if the deal didn't pan out, the Acostas would lose their home and everything they had. Holzer replied:

> 'Bernice, there is no doubt in my mind that this thing just can't miss, because the distribution arrangements for the film are all set with Warner Brothers, and as soon as we

deliver the film to them, they will pay us around $100,000 as "front money" and you will have 80% of your investment back right then. And it won't be long after that that it will all be back and then it's all gravy. I guarantee you will triple your money. I am sure that no one can lose anything.'

"21. At the same time and place, plaintiff Bernice Acosta asked Holzer whether there was a contract with Warner Brothers covering the above arrangement. Holzer replied that there was not yet a written contract, but that he would have one drafted and ready at the time the film was completed.

"22. The truth or falsity of the material representations of fact in Paragraph 20 above were matters peculiarly within the knowledge of Holzer, the plaintiffs not having access to such information.

"23. The above representations were false.

"24. Plaintiffs state on information and belief that the above representations were made by Holzer with intent to deceive and defraud the Acostas by inducing them to rely upon said representations to invest in the venture, and that Holzer knew the representations were false at the time they were made.

" * * *

"32. Holzer owned a substantial amount of stock in MPCA and a substantial interest in End Of Innocence, although he invested no cash of his own in the venture. His expectations of personal profit were directly dependent upon the Acostas making their substantial cash investment."

The complaint further alleges that Holzer, as attorney for plaintiffs, "then formed and organized plaintiff Pompei Del Lago Company, an Illinois corporation, the sole assets being the aforementioned Wisconsin real estate, the sole shareholders being the Acostas." Thereupon, the corporation, Pompei Del Lago Company, executed a $60,000 note, payable to Joseph G. Engert of the Northwestern Finance Company, secured by a second mortgage on the Wisconsin real estate, payable at the end of a year, with 6% interest. "$10,000 of the proceeds of the loan was retained by Engert as 'commission' on the loan, and $50,000 paid over by Engert to the Acostas personally, who in turn immediately paid it over to Holzer for 50,000 shares of stock of MPCA and $40,000 Limited Partnership

interest in End Of Innocence Company, all in the name of Bernice Acosta. This stock and limited partnership interest was immediately transferred to Engert as additional security on the loan. In addition, the note of Pompei Del Lago Company was personally guaranteed by the Acostas."

Upon completion of the film, plaintiffs "learned that no distribution agreement or arrangement with Warner Brothers or anyone else existed, and that no one was committed to pay MPCA 'front money' of around $100,000 or any other amount upon receipt of the film," which "was a complete flop * * * and the Acostas' interests therein are worthless."

Plaintiffs further allege that they are currently liable on the $60,000 note, and that the mortgage securing this note is being foreclosed. They allege damages "in the amount of $60,000, plus 6% interest from October 12, 1961."

An opinion of the trial court, included in the report of proceedings, contains a detailed review of the proceedings and a discussion of the arguments of counsel and applicable authorities, and shows that the action was considered as "a claim for a tort at law. It is not an action in equity." The court concluded that Counts I and II "do not state a cause of action at law as to the defendant, Holzer," and dismissed the action.

Defendant Holzer contends: (1) The complaint does not state a cause of action in fraud and deceit. It does not allege a misrepresentation of material existing facts. (2) There are no special circumstances here which convert a non-actionable statement into a fraudulent misrepresentation of a material existing fact. (3) The trial court properly held that no fiduciary relation existed between the parties.

In support of the contention that the complaint "does not allege a misrepresentation of material existing facts," defendant cites: Hayes v. Disque, 401 Ill. 479, 82 N.E.2d 350 (1948), at p. 488:

> "The charges of misrepresentation and deception in the present case are based upon statements relative to future or contingent events, expectations and probabilities, rather than upon present or pre-existing facts. Such statements do not generally constitute fraudulent misrepresentation or deceit but are regarded as mere expression of opinion or mere promises or conjectures upon which the other party has no right to rely. * * * In short, a charge of misrepresentation must be predicated upon statements of fact, rather than mere expression of opinion or prophesy."

Plavec v. Plavec, 30 Ill. App.2d 345, 174 N.E.2d 578 (1961), at p. 349:

> "Generally, a misrepresentation to constitute fraud must relate to a past or existing fact and not to the future. Actionable fraud ordinarily cannot be predicated upon a mere failure to perform a promise, even though there was no intention to perform the promise when it was made."

Schmidt v. Landfield, 20 Ill.2d 89, 169 N.E.2d 229 (1960), at p. 94:

> "As a general rule one who is guilty of fraudulent misrepresentation cannot interpose a defense that the person defrauded was negligent in failing to discover the truth. * * * The general rule is subject to the qualification, however, that the party seeking relief had a right to rely upon the representation made. * * * This court has pointed out accordingly that 'In all cases where it is sought to hold one liable for false representations, the question necessarily arises, whether, under all circumstances, the plaintiff had a right to rely upon them. In determining this question, the representations must be viewed in the light of all the facts of which the plaintiff had actual notice, and also of such as he might have availed himself by the exercise of ordinary prudence.' * * * The rule is well established that a party is not justified in relying on representations made when he has ample opportunity to ascertain the truth of the representations before he acts. When he is afforded the opportunity of knowing the truth of the representations he is chargeable with knowledge; and if he does not avail himself of the means of knowledge open to him he cannot be heard to say he

was deceived by misrepresentations."

Plaintiffs' authorities on materiality and reliance include Prosser on Torts, 2d Ed. (1955); 19 I.L.P., Fraud; and 37 C.J.S., Fraud, §§ 10 and 11. In Prosser, it is said (p. 554):

> "The party deceived must not only be justified in his belief that the representation is true, but he must also be justified in taking action on that basis. * * * There are misstatements which are so trivial, or so far unrelated to anything of real importance in the transaction, that the plaintiff will not be heard to say that they substantially affected his decision. Necessarily the test must be an objective one, and it cannot be stated in the form of any definite rule, but must depend upon the circumstances of the transaction itself."

At p. 555:

> "On the other hand facts to which a reasonable man might be expected to attach importance in making his choice of action, such as the identity of the directors of a corporation, the character of stock sold as treasury stock, * * *, the solvency of purchasers, the limited number of persons whose biographies are to be published in a book, * * *, have been held to be material. <u>The question is frequently for the jury whether the statement made might justifiably induce the action taken.</u>" [Emphasis supplied.]

At p. 556:

> "Justifiable reliance, of course, is essential to any form of relief for misrepresentation. It is more correct to say, therefore, that a statement of opinion is a representation of a fact, but of an immaterial fact, on which the law will not permit the opposing party to rely. When, for any reason, such reliance is regarded as reasonable and permissible, a misstatement of opinion may be a sufficient basis for relief."

At p. 561:

> "The courts have developed numerous exceptions to the rule that misrepresentations of opinion are not a basis for relief. Apparently all of these may be summed up by saying that they involve situations where special circumstances make it very reasonable or probable that the plaintiff should accept the defendant's opinion and act upon it, and so justify a relaxation of the distrust which is considered admirable between bargaining opponents. <u>Thus where</u>

> the parties stand in a relation of trust and confidence, as in the case of members of the same family, partners, attorney and client, * * *, and the like, it is held that reliance upon an opinion, whether it be as to a fact or a matter of law, is justifiable, and relief is granted." [Emphasis supplied.]

In 19 I.L.P., Fraud, § 14, p. 577, it is said:

> "The law, however, does not require more than that which is reasonable under the circumstances, with respect to the diligence which a plaintiff must employ. Thus, in the absence of circumstances putting a reasonable person on inquiry, a person is justified in relying on a misrepresentation of a material fact without making further inquiry.
>
> "Where positive statements are made in a manner not calculated to cause inquiry, or where there is intentional fraud, the mere presence of opportunities for investigation will not of itself preclude the right of reliance.
>
> "Where statements of matters of material fact concern matters which may be assumed to be within the knowledge of the party making them, the party to whom they are made may rely on them and need not make inquiries for himself in the absence of suspicious circumstances. The rule applies to a vendor's representations to a purchaser, and especially so where the property in question is located at a distance." [Emphasis supplied.]

Examining Count I of the amended complaint in the light of the foregoing authorities and pronouncements, we believe reasonable men might have difficulty in concluding that the statement, "the distribution arrangements for the film are all set with Warner Brothers, and as soon as we deliver the film to them, they will pay us around $100,000 as 'front money,'" should be considered only as "optimistic expressions of future expectations made by defendant in his enthusiasm over the future prospects of the film which had not yet even gone into production." We believe that this statement was a representation of an existing fact. Taken in context, the statement that "distribution arrangements are all set" could reasonably be considered as a representation that there was an oral contract in

existence, or, at least, that an "arrangement" had been entered into with Warner Brothers for the distribution of the film when it was completed. Although the $100,000 was to be paid in the future, the oral contract or arrangement itself had a present existence.

We do not believe that the allegations of paragraph 21 of the complaint "qualify or take away from the force of the representations" alleged to have been made in paragraph 20. We cannot agree with defendant that Holzer's alleged reply to Bernice Acosta's question made it "clear that this was something which was not yet agreed to but remained to be consummated in the future." Holzer's reply did not deny the existence of an oral contract, nor the existence of "arrangements," and may be reasonably construed to imply an affirmative response to these possibilities.

We also believe that the statements alleged in paragraph 20 of the complaint were "material." Among other statements, Holzer allegedly represented that "you will have 80% of your investment back right then." The statements allegedly made, considering the circumstances of the transaction, are not "so trivial, or so far unrelated to anything of real importance in the transaction, that the plaintiff[s] will not be heard to say that they substantially affected [their] decision."

Defendant further contends that plaintiffs had no right to rely on his representations--"What person of any ordinary intelligence would rely on these statements as meaning that firm agreements had been made on a film which no one had seen because it had not even been made! Who would really believe that a film company had agreed to pay $100,000 for a film to be made in the future!" Defendant further argues that "[i]f they did believe and rely upon these statements to relate to existing facts, then they were grossly

negligent in not investigating before investing." Defendant goes on to state that "There are no allegations that defendant in any way sought to discourage or hinder them from inquiring anywhere or from investigating. No trip to California was necessary. An ordinary letter would have confirmed defendant's statement that he had no contract with Warner Brothers at the time but that they contemplated completing arrangements when they saw the film. A telephone call would have achieved the same result."

We believe it should first be made clear as to what representation the plaintiffs allege they justifiably relied upon. They do not allege reliance on any representation as to a written contract with Warner Brothers. Plaintiffs relied, rather, on the representation that "distribution arrangements for the film are all set." We think the complaint alleges sufficient facts to show that plaintiffs, under the circumstances, were justified, without making further inquiry, in relying on this alleged misrepresentation of this material fact. Plaintiffs' conduct was not unreasonable in the light of their earlier relationship of attorney and client, wherein Holzer had graciously refused to charge them for his services. Plaintiffs reasonably could have developed sufficient trust and confidence in defendant, a prominent lawyer, to accept his statement on a matter about which he professed to have superior knowledge and special information and which he had investigated for two years. The plaintiffs alleged that prior to the aviation venture, they "had no experience in business or investments." These factors, and others, lead us to the conclusion that plaintiffs were not dealing with defendant at arm's length or on equal terms.

There is nothing alleged in the complaint that could be characterized as "suspicious circumstances" which would put a

reasonable person in the same situation on inquiry, even if the principle that "one cannot impute negligence as against his own deliberate fraud" is not applied. Roda v. Berko, 401 Ill. 335, 342, 81 N.E.2d 912 (1948). We find the complaint alleges facts sufficient to show justifiable reliance.

We next consider whether the complaint contained the remaining elements of fraud and deceit--falsity, scienter, deception and injury. Although the amended complaint is to be construed most strongly against plaintiffs, they are entitled to the reasonable intendments of the language used. (Field v. Oberwortmann, 14 Ill. App.2d 218, 220, 144 N.E.2d 637 (1957).) Under the Civil Practice Act, pleadings are to be liberally construed with a view toward doing substantial justice between the parties, and no pleading is to be deemed bad in substance which shall contain such information as shall reasonably inform the opposite party of the nature of the claim. (Crosby v. Weil, 382 Ill. 538, 548, 48 N.E.2d 386 (1943).) The pleader should allege the ultimate facts to be proved and not allege the evidentiary facts which tend to prove the ultimate facts. (Levinson v. Home Bank & Trust Co., 337 Ill. 241, 244, 169 N.E. 193 (1929).) "There is no clear distinction between statements of 'evidentiary facts,' 'ultimate facts,' and 'conclusions of law.' There is no provision in the Civil Practice Act defining a conclusion, and a precise definition as to what constitutes conclusions of law is impossible." Nichols, Illinois Civil Practice, Revised Edition, (1961), Vol. 2, § 777, p. 27.

Using these pleading guidelines, we find the complaint does allege ultimate facts sufficient to charge the remaining elements of fraud. Paragraph 23 alleges the material representations "were false." This is an ultimate fact which plaintiffs must prove, and

the statement gives defendant reasonable notice of the nature of the charge.

As to "scienter," paragraph 24 alleges, "Holzer knew the representations were false at the time they were made." This allegation is made on information and belief, which "is not equivalent to an allegation of relevant fact." (Whitley v. Frazier, 21 Ill.2d 292, 294, 171 N.E.2d 644 (1961).) However, we believe it is sufficient here. It alleges a fact peculiarly within defendant Holzer's knowledge, and plaintiffs are not required to allege with precision "facts which are, to a much greater degree of exactitude, within the knowledge of defendant rather than of plaintiffs." Opal v. Material Service Corp., 9 Ill. App.2d 433, 441, 133 N.E.2d 733 (1956).

The allegations in paragraphs 20 to 24 are sufficient to charge deception and require no discussion. "Injury" is demonstrated, and damages are alleged in exact figures.

Although we express no opinion on the merits of this case, we hold that Count I, standing alone, is sufficient to state a cause of action for fraud and deceit and, accordingly, should be answered.

For the reasons given, the order striking the second amended complaint and dismissing the action as to defendant Holzer is reversed, and the cause is remanded for further proceedings consistent with the views expressed herein.

REVERSED AND REMANDED WITH DIRECTIONS.

KLUCZYNSKI, J., concurs.

BURMAN, P.J., dissenting:

I an unable to concur in the foregoing decision. The complaint in question clearly shows that the plaintiffs, the defendant and other persons invested jointly in a venture to promote the production of a documentary film on the subject of Communism. Everyone, including the defendant, hoped to make "bundles" of money, but, unfortunately, the venture proved unsuccessful. Although the defendant is not charged with obtaining the plaintiffs' money for his own personal gain and although he is not charged with selling his stock and keeping the plaintiffs' money, the plaintiffs seek to recoup their lost investment by charging the defendant with causing them to invest in the enterprise through false representations. I do not believe that the complaint states a cause of action for fraud. Rather the complaint seeks, in effect, to hold the defendant liable as a guarantor of the plaintiffs' investment.

A complaint alleging fraud must state sufficient acts or facts to establish the fraud. Tate v. Jackson, 22 Ill. App. 2d 471, 161 N.E.2d 156; Neboshek v. Berzani, 42 Ill. App. 2d 220, 191 N.E.2d 411. One of the elements which it is necessary to allege in order to properly plead a case of fraud is that the defendant's false representations on which the plaintiff relied were representations concerning a material past or existing fact; it is not sufficient to allege that the defendant made a promise to do some act in the future (Brodsky v. Frank, 342 Ill. 110, 173 N.E. 775; Sinclair v. Sullivan Chevrolet Co., 31 Ill. 2d 507, 202 N.E.2d 516) and it is not sufficient to allege that the defendant made a representation concerning future or contingent events, expectations or probabilities (Hayes v. Disque, 401 Ill. 479, 82 N.E.2d 350; Keithley v. Mutual Life Ins. Co., 271 Ill. 584, 111 N.E. 503).

The crux of the plaintiffs' case is contained in paragraphs twenty through twenty-four of their amended complaint. The representations principally relied on are contained in paragraphs twenty and twenty-one. Paragraph twenty-two alleges that the truth or falsity of the representations were matters peculiarly within the knowledge of the defendant; paragraph twenty-three alleges that the representations were false; and paragraph twenty-four alleges that the representations were made by the defendant with the intent to deceive and defraud the plaintiffs and that the defendant knew the representations to be false. The only representations alleged to have been made by the defendant were the following: that "large profits to the investors were a virtual certainty;" that "this thing just can't miss, because the distribution arrangements for the film are all set with Warner Brothers, and as soon as we deliver the film to them, they will pay us around $100,000 as 'front money' and you will have 80% of your investment back right then. And it won't be long after that that it will all be back and then its all gravy. I guarantee you will triple your money. I am sure that no one can lose anything;" and that when he spoke to the plaintiffs about investing "there was not yet a written contract [with Warner Brothers], but that he would have one drafted and ready at the time the film was completed."

In my opinion none of the above statements, except that concerning the distribution arrangements, were representations concerning material past or existing facts. They were either promises to do acts in the future or they were representations concerning future or contingent events, expectations or probabilities which cannot serve as the basis of an action for fraud.

Although the complaint alleges one material existing fact,

that is, that "distribution arrangements for the film are all set with Warner Brothers," I believe that the rule in Schmidt v. Landfield, 20 Ill. 2d 89, 169 N.E.2d 229, applies and the plaintiffs cannot rely on that representation alone to support their action. In Schmidt it was said:

> This court has pointed out accordingly that "In all cases where it is sought to hold one liable for false representations, the question necessarily arises, whether, under all the circumstances, the plaintiff had a right to rely upon them. In determining this question, the representations must be viewed in the light of all the facts of which the plaintiff had actual notice, and also of such as he might have availed himself by the exercise of ordinary prudence." (Dillman v. Nadlehoffer, 119 Ill. 567, 577.) The rule is well established that a party is not justified in relying on representations made when he has ample opportunity to ascertain the truth of the representations before he acts. When he is afforded the opportunity of knowing the truth of the representations he is chargeable with knowledge; and if he does not avail himself of the means of knowledge open to him he cannot be heard to say he was deceived by misrepresentations. [citing cases] (20 Ill. 2d at page 94)

It is evident from the complaint that when the plaintiffs joined the venture they knew that the film had not been completed, that there was no written contract with Warner Brothers, and that no written contract would even be drafted until after the film was produced at some time in the future. In short, the plaintiffs were on notice that they were investing only in the expectation of completing the film and of securing a successful deal to be entered into in the future. The only existing fact of which they had notice was that some kind of informal distribution arrangements had been "all set" with Warner Brothers. In these circumstances, the plaintiffs could easily have contacted Warner Brothers by letter or phone to ascertain the truth of the representation concerning distribution

arrangements. It is not alleged that the defendant discouraged them from doing this. Since the plaintiffs could easily have ascertained the truth of the only representation of a material existing fact which the defendant is alleged to have made, they are chargeable with knowledge of the truth and cannot now claim to have been deceived.

The plaintiffs argue that even if the alleged representations are not statements of material existing facts on which they could properly rely, the complaint states a cause of action because, first, it pleads certain special circumstances and, second, because the relationship of attorney and client existed between the defendant and the plaintiffs and hence the alleged representations were made by a fiduciary and were actionable fraud. I do not agree. The plaintiffs cite numerous cases in support of their first argument, but I believe that these cases are distinguishable from the present case and do not control it. A lengthy discussion of these cases would benefit neither party and would unduly lengthen this opinion. Moreover, in my judgment, no fiduciary relationship was involved here; rather the parties were co-investors in an enterprise that failed.

I would affirm the judgment of the Circuit Court dismissing the plaintiffs' amended complaint.

Lightning Source UK Ltd.
Milton Keynes UK
UKHW010757221218
334411UK00004B/220/P

9 780332 743110